Let's Go to Chicago!

Written and Illustrated by

KAREN DEAN

Copyright © 2004 Karen Dean all rights reserved.

Publisher's Cataloging-in-Publication
(Provided by Quality Books, Inc.)

Dean, Karen (Karen Tanielian)
   Let's go to Chicago! / written and illustrated by Karen Dean.
     p.cm. -- (Let's go! ; 2)
     SUMMARY: Come along to Chicago with the Butler family and experience the museums, tall buildings, Navy Pier, Lincoln Park Zoo boat rides and much more.
     ISBN 1-928623-43-3

     1. Chicago (Ill.)--Description and travel--Juvenile literature. 2. Chicago (Ill.)--History--Juvenile literature. 3. Chicago (Ill.)--Description and travel. 4. Chicago (Ill.)--History.   I. Title. II. Title: Chicago.

F548.33.D43 2004   917.73'11044
                              QBI04-700303

Dedication:
With love to my daughters and their husbands,
Trisha (Matt) and Tracy (Art),
and to my Mom, Jane.
Thank you for all your love and support.

Acknowledgments

Thanks to:
Duncan Jaenicke for editorial expertise and
First Page Publications for editing, marketing, and overall support.

Special thanks to
my husband, **Dave Dean**,
without whose help the books wouldn't happen.

"Woo-woooo!"

boomed the train's whistle

as the locomotive thundered

through the

street crossing,

warning people

to stay clear.

The shiny

steel wheels

of the train

rolled quickly

down the tracks,

making a

"clackety-clack"

at each crossing,

then settling into a peaceful hum

as they sped swiftly through the countryside.

The train stopped from time to time at small towns and suburbs to pick up new passengers.

Finally, the train was approaching Chicago, "The Windy City."

Mom and 6-year-old Jessie—his eyes glued to the window—had followed their journey on the map all the way from home, carefully checking off each city they passed.

Travis, age 9, pretended he didn't care.

How could we possibly have fun on a vacation without Dad?

he thought to himself, pouting. Almost a year ago, Mom and Dad had divorced. Travis was still trying to accept that big change in their lives. Now rolling through Chicago neighborhoods, they saw tightly-packed houses leading up to downtown where super-tall buildings, called "skyscrapers," reached up to kiss the sky.

Their train somehow magically navigated the confusing web of train tracks that led to the dark,

cave-like train station. Trains were coming and going in all directions.

With a mighty lurch and a loud "Skreeech!" their train finally came to a stop.

The boys' hearts started beating faster—at long last, they had arrived!

Mom, too, took a deep breath—she wondered if she could manage everything alone,

now that she was single again.

The boys had waited for what seemed like years for this day to arrive.

From brochures Mom got from the travel agent, they had carefully planned their sightseeing beforehand. Mom had eagerly looked forward to her week off from work. She anticipated lots of fun time with her boys, a time to bond, and to build family memories. She hoped Travis' bad mood wouldn't spoil their special adventure together.

7

Grabbing their luggage, they walked *up* to the street

(Chicago's train station is built underneath its busy streets).

As they ventured into the bright sunlight, the city was absolutely alive with excitement.

Everywhere they looked, cars, buses and people were in a hurry to get somewhere,

weaving their way through the forest of tall buildings

that now surrounded them.

Overwhelmed, Jessie clutched Mom's hand and asked, "How will we ever find our hotel?"

Mom assured him,

"We'll take a taxi to the hotel—the taxi driver knows his way around.

It's extremely important that we always stick close together.

I need your help to be extra obedient,

so no one will get lost."

"Okay, Mom," both boys agreed.

The thought of getting lost in Chicago was pretty scary.

They walked to the taxi stand, climbed in, and zoomed off.

After quickly settling into their hotel, they decided to visit the first place on their list, Sears Tower. How to get there? Should they take the bus, taxi, trolley bus, or elevated train? All the choices seemed so attractive that the boys couldn't decide, so Mom chose the trolley bus.

"Will we go shopping at Sears Tower?" asked Jessie.

He remembered the Sears store back home, with its huge toy section.

"Jessie," said Travis in a frustrated tone of voice, "The Sears Tower isn't a store, it's an office building—one of the tallest in the world," as if a six-year-old should already know that.

"Look," said Travis, pointing in the distance. "You can see it from here. It's taller than all the other buildings."

They got off the trolley bus and began walking

to the base of the gigantic building,

which occupies an entire city block.

"The Sears Tower is 110 stories high," said Travis,

always acting like a tour guide.

"Are they scary stories?

Will I have nightmares?" worried Jessie.

Mom smiled and explained,

" 'Stories' means floors, or levels, of a building.

From the very top floor—called the Sky Deck—you can see four

different states on a clear day:

Wisconsin, Illinois, Indiana and Michigan."

"Can we go see?" asked Jessie,

tilting his head way back, to see the top.

"We'll do that later," said Mom.

"Let's look at the map to see where we get the water taxi right now.

It's going to take us on a tour, and then end at the museums."

When Jessie heard about the water taxi, he almost jumped out of his shoes, squealing with delight.

Jessie had gone sailing with Grandpa last summer and talked about it all year long.

They walked to the Chicago River, down some steps to the dock,

and climbed aboard the water taxi.

The big boat whooshed down the Chicago River,

sometimes riding smoothly, other times bouncing on top of the waves.

The sun peeked at them from between the tall buildings,

disappearing occasionally when they passed under massive bridges.

Most of the bridges held cars and people; others allowed trains to cross the water.

"Chicago has the second largest train system in America," explained Mom.

"Every workday, more than 1.7 million people go to work and

then home again aboard commuter trains.

Since the trains end up circling downtown Chicago, they call it the Loop.

Instead of fighting traffic, folks can read, talk on the phone, or take a nap."

The boys couldn't imagine sleeping on a train—to them it was too exciting a place to snooze!

While they cruised the river,

a tour guide pointed out architectural styles,

but the boys weren't listening.

Jessie imagined Grandpa as captain of the water taxi, and

Travis wondered about the yucky fishy smell coming off the water.

"Each spring for Saint Patrick's Day, the city of Chicago turns the river green, using tons of dye,"

explained Travis to his little brother.

"They turn the whole river green? No way!" challenged Jessie.

"You're trying to trick me!"

Mom smiled knowingly at the playful rivalry between her sons.

Travis pointed, boasting, "Look—it's right here in this brochure."

"Oh," said Jessie quietly.

As their boat putt-putted along,
    Mom pointed out Navy Pier
        with its Ferris Wheel, carousel, and
            other fun-looking rides.
                Some really huge boats
                    were parked at the dock there.
                        "Mom!" shouted Jessie.
                            "I want to stop and ride the rides!"
                              Mom, not swayed by Jessie's impulsiveness,
                                replied, "Don't worry,
                                  we'll be back to Navy Pier soon, boys."

Finally, the water taxi let them off in front of the Shedd Aquarium, where they boarded a shuttle to the Museum of Science and Industry. The museum was filled with interesting exhibits to please everyone: displays about history, technology, and health. One room had full-sized trains, and planes hanging from the ceiling. Both boys wished they could climb up into those planes.

Jessie asked, "Mom, can I fly one of those planes over to Grandpa's house?"

"Not today," smiled Mom, winking at Travis.

Mom studied the museum's map to find out which exhibit came next.

When she looked up, Jessie was gone.

She urgently asked Travis where his little brother was.

"He was saying something about weird-looking cars around that corner," explained Travis.

They hurried to the next gallery, and caught Jessie climbing into the front seat of a Model-T Ford.

Mom was relieved, but also a bit embarrassed to have to shoo Jessie off the displays!

They looked at many exhibits, but didn't have time to see everything.

They experienced a jet plane ride, toured a coal mine, and learned what the Space Shuttle is all about.

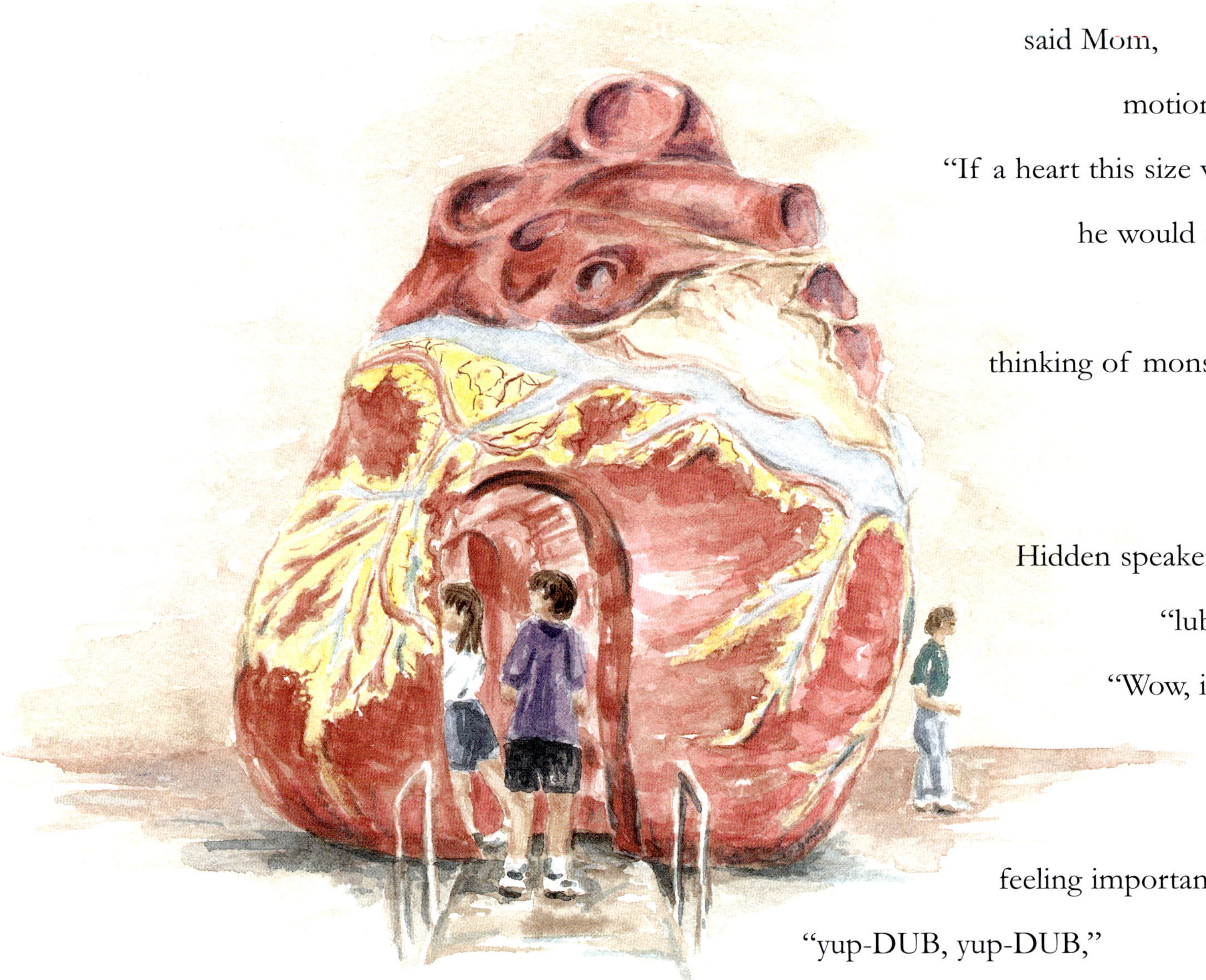

"Let's walk through this giant heart,"

said Mom,

motioning for the boys to follow.

"If a heart this size were in a real person,

he would stand 28 stories tall."

Jessie's eyes bugged out,

thinking of monster movies he had seen.

"Listen to the heartbeat, Jessie,"

said Travis.

Hidden speakers inside the model repeated:

"lub-DUB, lub-DUB."

"Wow, is that what my heart sounds like?"

asked Jessie.

"Yup," said Travis,

feeling important and scientific.

"yup-DUB, yup-DUB,"

he mimicked with a grin.

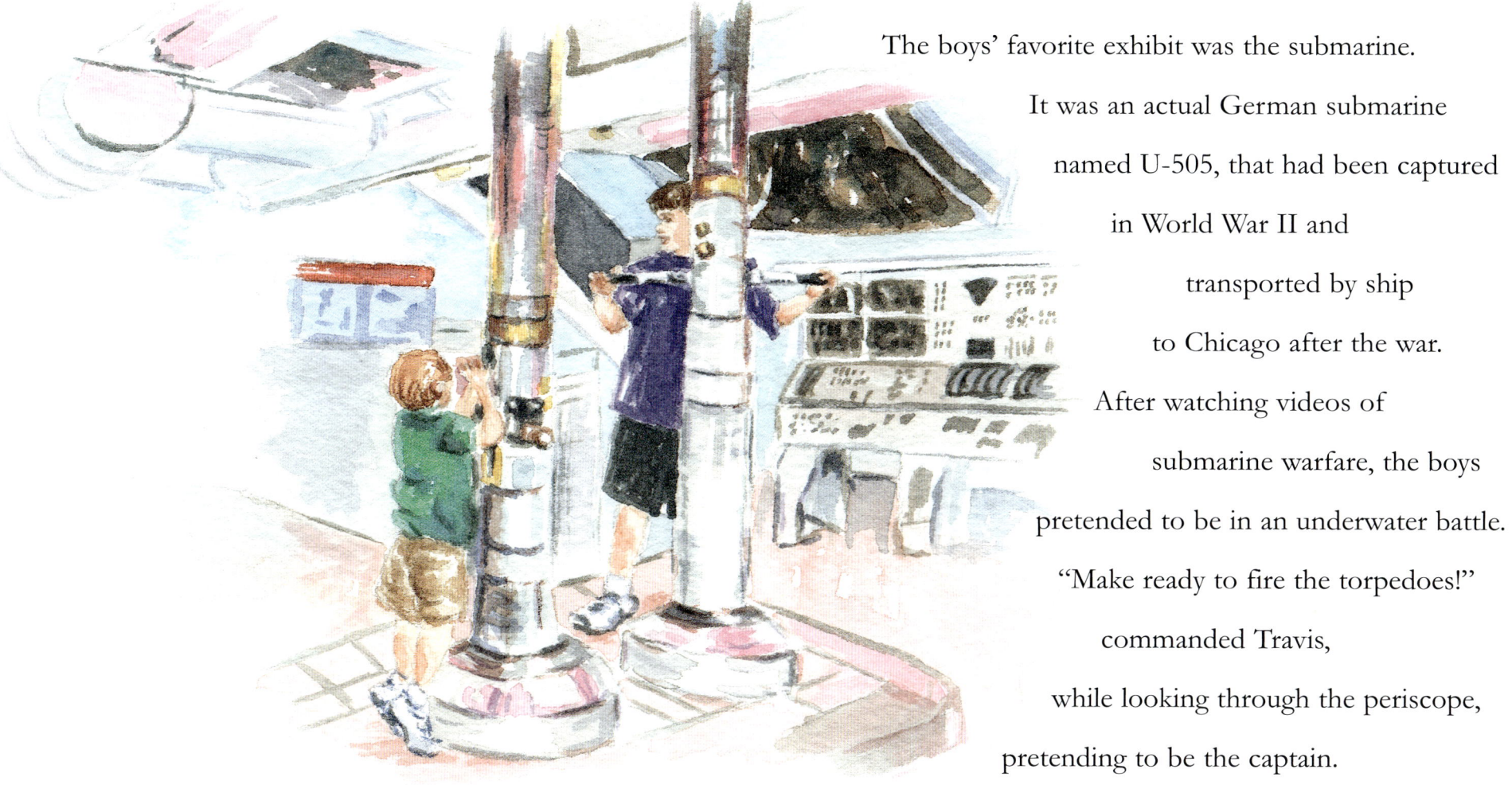

The boys' favorite exhibit was the submarine. It was an actual German submarine named U-505, that had been captured in World War II and transported by ship to Chicago after the war. After watching videos of submarine warfare, the boys pretended to be in an underwater battle. "Make ready to fire the torpedoes!" commanded Travis, while looking through the periscope, pretending to be the captain.

"What's a torpedo?" asked Jessie, puzzled.

Travis chuckled and explained, then showed his little brother which lever to pull to shoot the torpedoes at the enemy ships!

Looking on, it seemed to Mom that Travis might actually be having fun.

Was that a smile she saw creeping onto his face?

"Okay boys," said Mom.

"That's all the time we have for this museum.

Now we're going to the Field Museum of Natural History."

"Is that where the dinosaurs are?" squealed Jessie with delight.

"It sure is," said Mom with a big grin, knowing how much Jessie loved dinosaurs.

On the shuttle ride over, Mom reviewed the brochure and explained:

"We'll be learning about animals, birds, plants, rocks, fossils, and

how people from other cultures lived long ago.

You'll have many interesting things to talk about when you go back to school."

"I mostly just want to see the dinosaurs," said Jessie.

As soon as they entered the museum, both boys ran into the huge room to see the enormous *Tyrannosaurus Rex* named Sue.

Feeling a mixture of excitement combined with a little fear, they carefully checked out Sue from every angle.

"I wish I could touch it," whispered Jessie mischievously.

"You'd better not—you already got in trouble with that old car," scolded Travis.

"Sue was 42 feet long and weighed 14,000 pounds when she walked the earth, millions of years ago," instructed Mom. "She was a meat-eater, at the top of the food chain—meaning that she was so strong and fierce that no other dinosaurs would dare attack her."

Jessie was sure glad that dinosaurs like Sue don't walk around anymore!

Travis was the most interested

in the glowing display cases showing tools, dwellings, clothing, and weapons

of North American Indians from long ago.

"How could people live in these places?" questioned Travis.

"When it's the only life you know, then it seems perfectly normal," explained Mom.

She told the boys about Chicago's early history:

it was written about by French Catholic missionary

Father Jacques Marquette and Canadian explorer Louis Jolliet in 1673.

"Can we be done here yet?" complained Jessie. "Where are the other dinosaurs anyways?"

"Look at the map with me, Jessie," said Mom. "Help me find the other dinosaur fossils."

"This is really weird," said Jessie,

slowly walking through the eerie,

dimly-lit displays with dinosaur bones

surrounding him.

"Just think how scary it would be

if all of these dinosaurs were alive

right here, right now,"

said Travis in a spooky voice,

trying to freak out Jessie.

He continued,

louder, while rushing up behind Jessie,

"…and what if THEY ALL STARTED CHASING AFTER YOU!!!"

Travis dug his fingernails, like mock claws, into his brother's back.

"Stop it!" screamed Jessie, jumping,

trying hard not to show he was afraid.

"Mom! Travis is being mean!"

Mom, trying not to laugh,

gave Travis a fierce look that made him stop.

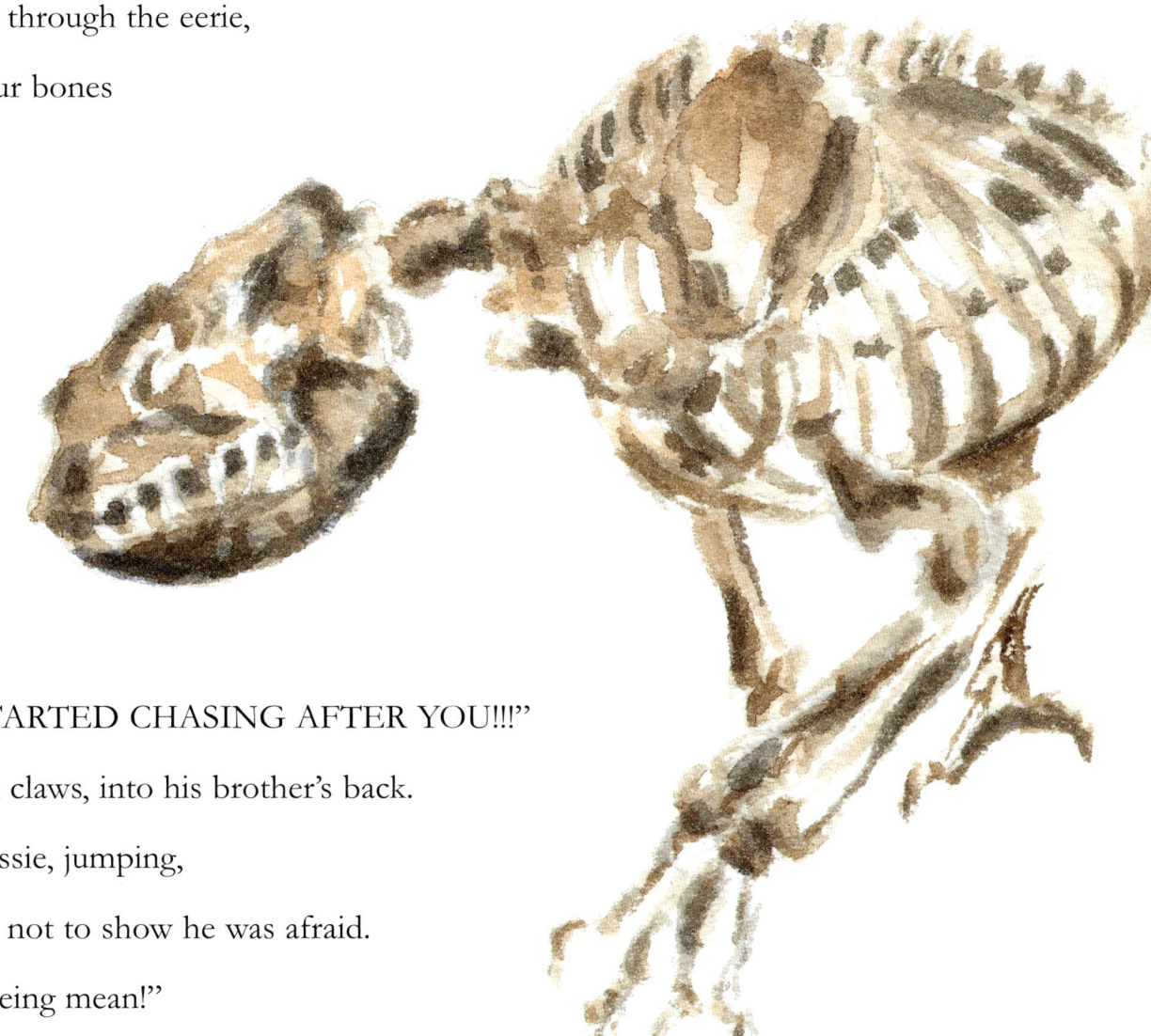

They stayed longest in the room that displayed enormous dinosaur fossils, along with drawings of how the dinosaurs might have looked when they were alive. Fossils, Mom explained, are impressions in rock of ancient animals, or parts of animals—like the jawbone of a sabre-toothed tiger. Even though the actual animal has died and rotted away, we can see a "picture" of them in these rock-hard impressions that remain. Scientists around the world dig up fossils—and sometimes even boys and girls can find them in the dirt or at the beach. Mom explained that the Tyrannosaurus Rex the boys saw when they first entered the museum was named after an amateur fossil hunter named Sue, who discovered the bones in 1990 in South Dakota. It is the largest and most complete Tyrannosaurus Rex ever discovered in the world.

Jessie wanted to know the name of *every* dinosaur. He pushed several buttons on the displays to hear the names out loud, then kept repeating them over and over again, so he wouldn't forget.

"Apatosaurus, Tyrannosaurus, Hadrosaurus, Proto…um, something, Tricer…something."

"We need to go now," said Mom.

"Just a few more minutes, please," begged Jessie. "Now, what was that name again?"

"I've had enough museums for today," sighed Mom. "Let's go outside now."

"Sounds good to me," said Travis. "Me too," agreed Jessie reluctantly.

He trailed along behind, gazing back at the dinosaurs for as long as he could,

mumbling as many of their names as he could remember.

Burnham Park Harbor was the perfect place to sit and relax outside while getting something to eat.

The boats gently bobbed about on the rippling water, while the tall,

hazy buildings across the park

reminded them that they were still in Chicago.

Up in the park, not far from the boats, people were enjoying the activity of Buckingham Fountain.

The water seemed to dance to a frolicking beat, bubbling out of spouts, and foaming over curves.

Mom explained that all these attractions are part of a magnificent lakeside park that stretches about five miles along the shoreline of Lake Michigan, making Chicago's downtown one of America's most beautiful.

Jessie's focus was still on the sailboats in the harbor, wishing he was on one sailing to the middle of Lake Michigan. Instead, they took a quick ride on the water taxi back to Navy Pier, where they would discover a very different kind of fountain.

Children were having a great time splashing in the water of the unpredictable fountain at Navy Pier.

Instead of water flowing continuously from the holes, water would start squirting—or stop—without warning.

Children happily played in the fountain.

"Mom, can I go play in the water?" begged Jessie.

"Sorry, Jessie, but you can't get your clothes all wet.

You'd need a bathing suit," explained Mom.

Though disappointed,

Jessie still

had fun

watching the

unpredictable

water spouts

surprise the

children.

"Ping!

That girl got it

right in her face,"

he giggled.

28

There was way more to see and do at Navy Pier than they had expected, including a pirate who pretended his hat was a funny talking parrot; the 'parrot' sang in a hilarious voice, complete with loud, startling SQUAWKS!

The pirate told of his journeys in search of buried treasure.

He juggled shiny pirate swords—without getting cut.

Then, Mom, Travis and Jessie soared high up in the air on the giant Ferris Wheel. They could see far, far away, which was thrilling—but all the same, it was good to come down again. Jessie was afraid of heights!

In a rush to get off the ferris wheel, Jessie stumbled, fell, and scraped his knee.

Travis rushed to pick him up, and then comforted his crying brother.

Mom was delighted to see Travis being so helpful and caring for his brother.

"Let's take a bus to our hotel now, boys. Would anyone be interested in getting a deep dish Chicago pizza for dinner?"

They both nodded in agreement.

The pizza gave them enough energy to walk around for a little while. Evening was the perfect time to lean over the railing on the bridge, just watching the boats slowly cruising down the river and the sun reflecting off the tall buildings in the distance. It was a sharp contrast to the big city traffic right behind them. They were extremely tired from all their sightseeing, and so decided to take a taxi back to their hotel to settle down for the night.

"Let's get to sleep early," said Mom. "There will be much more to see tomorrow."

The boys were too exhausted to even respond, and within minutes they were fast asleep.

When they awoke the next morning, it was pouring down rain.

"Does this mean we can't take the water taxi?" asked Jessie. "And what about the zoo?"

"We can take the bus instead," comforted Mom.

"But I wanted to ride the boat again," whined Jessie.

"Who knows?" said Mom. "Maybe the weather will clear up."

Sure enough, as they were eating breakfast, the sky *did* start clearing up.

"See, Jessie?" said Travis. "You were griping for nothing."

They took the water taxi after all, heading for the Museum Campus.

Suddenly, a huge water cannon shot a rainbow of water across the river,

causing boats from both directions to quickly stop,

so the passengers wouldn't get wet.

"What's happening?" shouted Travis, within earshot of the boat's captain.

The captain explained, "The water is arched across,

as a reminder of when the flow of the Chicago River was reversed

in 1900 to improve the quality of the water, making it safer to drink."

"Boys, where do you want to go first today?" asked Mom.

"Will it be the Adler Planetarium or the Shedd Aquarium?"

"Planetarium," said Travis quickly, before Jessie even had a chance to think.

They were enjoying the boat ride, leaning on the railing, watching all the tall buildings pass by. Suddenly, Travis pointed to a dark shape in the water and shouted, "Jessie, look out! It's a crocodile!"

Jessie jumped back in panic.

Then he noticed Travis laughing hilariously. Mom was chuckling, too.

Just to make things worse, people sitting nearby were laughing also.

"That's not funny!" protested Jessie, all flustered.

Then he cautiously peeked over the side of the boat again. "That's just a stupid stick," Jessie complained to his big brother.

"No kidding. There aren't any crocodiles in Chicago—it's too cold here," chuckled Travis.

Visiting the Adler Planetarium was like entering a completely different universe.

The boys became lost in their thoughts,

imagining themselves traveling in space while studying the Milky Way Galaxy, the sun, and the planets.

The boys checked out a big blue sphere that, when spun, looks like Earth's atmosphere in motion.

Depending on how fast or slow it goes, it looks like the swirls that planets create as they zoom through space.

They next stopped at the Shedd Aquarium,

where they saw many varieties of fish in small and medium-sized tanks.

Then, there was one enormous tank where the diver gets right in with the fish to feed them.

"That's the biggest fish tank I ever saw," said Jessie. He went from one window to another,

following one huge fish that was swimming

around colorful

coral and waving

seaweed. He was

so focused on the

journey of the fish

that—not wanting to

lose track of it—he

forgot his manners

and began pushing

his way in front

of other people.

"Careful Jessie,"

whispered Mom.

At the penguin exhibit, the playful penguins attracted a large crowd of visitors as they slid down rocks,

darted through the frigid water, then popped back up on the rocks again. Some waddled into a cozy corner.

Others huddled peacefully with newborn chicks tucked beneath them for warmth and protection.

One timid penguin stood at the water's edge for so long,

looking like he would dive in, but in the end "chickened out."

When a bothersome buddy waddled over,

poking and pestering him,

the poor penguin

climbed to a

higher rock

to be left alone.

The buddy

gave up and

dove in himself,

enjoying the

cold water

penguin

paradise.

After about two hours at Shedd Aquarium, when they went outside to leave,

Mom noticed a huge fog bank had rolled in off the lake.

Jessie noticed it, too, and told Mom,

"That fog looks like cotton candy trying to hide the tall buildings."

Travis asked Jessie if he realized that fog is actually very low clouds.

"I didn't know that," responded Jessie, impressed. "That's cool."

Navy Pier was next.

Riding the water taxi there for lunch,

the fog hid most of the rides.

But as their boat got closer, it became more clear.

"Who's hungry? asked Mom. The boys shot up their hands.

"Let's try the famous 'Chicago-style' hot dog, shall we?" suggested Mom.

"What's that?" asked Jessie.

"Well, it has a Vienna hot dog, mustard, relish, onions, hot peppers, pickles, tomatoes,

and a dash of celery salt. Does that sound good to you guys?" she asked.

"Just mustard on mine," said Jessie.

"I'll have mustard, ketchup, and relish on mine," said Travis.

"No hot peppers? You two are boring!" joked Mom.

"I'm going for the Chicago dog."

They were all pleased with their own choice.

Their plan was to go to the John Hancock building next,

and then the Sears Tower, but it was too foggy to see anything from so high up.

"We'll have to do something else now," said Mom. "I suggest the Lincoln Park Zoo."

"But you said we could go to the top," said Jessie.

"I know," said Mom. "But the fog would block our view.

We'll have to wait until tomorrow morning

and decide if we can fit those tall buildings in before we leave."

The shuttle ride to the zoo was a nice break, even though Jessie pouted most of the way.

But arriving at the colorful zoo on Lake Michigan improved his attitude quickly.

At the children's farm, the speckled,

clucking chickens were pecking everything in sight—including Jessie's hand.

"What are you doing?" asked Travis,

noticing a pen full of chickens around his little brother.

"It feels really funny," giggled Jessie.

The nearby paddleboats caught the boys' attention,

and seemed to be calling them to come ride,

but their excitement to see the animals at the main zoo was more important for now.

The monkeys put on a great show,

chasing each other around,

and hanging in silly ways from branches and ropes.

Enormous elephants threw dirt around with their trunks,

while camels walked around and around,

as if on an imaginary caravan to nowhere.

The bears weren't very friendly.

They just hid in the corners of the rocks.

Probably they were too hot on this summer day—or maybe just tired

of so many people who were staring at them,

and making funny noises that they couldn't understand.

After walking what seemed to Mom like 100 miles,

they decided they had had enough of the zoo.

"I'm hungry," exclaimed Travis,

drooping like he was weak from starvation.

"Can we eat at some restaurant with tables outside?"

"Great idea," agreed Mom. "I'm sure there is something nearby."

They walked a few blocks and found a nice restaurant

where they could rest their feet and enjoy the evening light outside.

They enjoyed recalling all the fun things they had experienced.

Then they went back to the hotel for their last night.

The next morning at breakfast, Mom asked,

"What should we do

during our last few hours in Chicago?

It's a beautiful sunny day—without fog—so I suggest

we start with the John Hancock Observatory.

What do you think, guys?"

"That's my first choice," agreed Travis.

"Me, too," said Jessie,

with renewed energy for the new day.

"I also want to window shop

a little on the Magnificent Mile," said Mom.

She explained that this stretch

of Michigan Avenue,

just north of the Chicago River,

is one of the most famous

shopping areas in the world.

There are hundreds of fabulous stores,

restaurants, galleries, and hotels.

On the way up to the Hancock Observatory,

Jessie and Travis held their hands over their ears in the elevator.

They soared up 94 floors so fast, it made their ears pop.

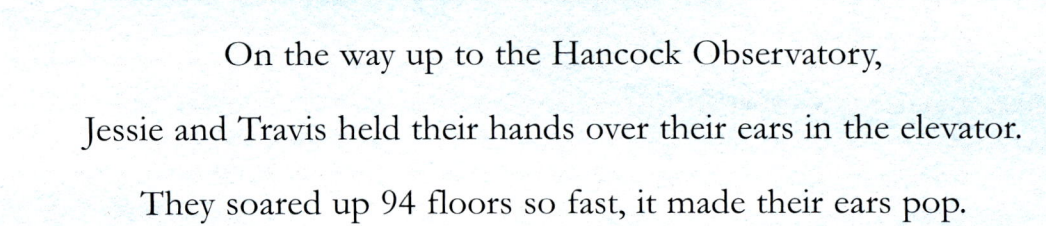

"You can see all around Chicago from this high up—and even into four states on a clear day," said Mom.

The observatory had floor-to-ceiling glass walls on all four sides of the building, a 360-degree view.

Pointing, Mom said, "Look—right over there is Navy Pier, and the Museum Campus is way over there. Can you find the Sears Tower? Remember, it's the tallest skyscraper, even taller than where we stand now."

"I see it!" boasted Travis.

"Where? Show me, show me!" said Jessie.

Travis, who enjoys geography in school, asked, "Mom, where are the four states?"

"Illinois is down below, of course." Mom said, pointing. "Indiana is to the southeast, over there; and Michigan begins a little to the east of Indiana, stretching up the other side of Lake Michigan, about 80 miles that way."

"Where is the fourth state?" asked Travis.

"Come with me," Mom said mysteriously, walking away from the boys.

They scrambled to catch up—where was she taking them?

They walked around to the north side of the observatory.

Pointing, Mom said, "Wisconsin is way up there; the border is about 40 miles away."

Mom and the boys spent a short time shopping on the Magnificent Mile, near the historic Water Tower.

The Water Tower is the only remaining structure after the Great Chicago Fire,

which, in 1871, destroyed almost all the buildings.

Back then, fire departments weren't very well equipped,

and the buildings were made entirely of wood, so fires quickly got out of control.

After shopping, they picked up their luggage from the hotel and hurried to the train station.

On the long ride home, they talked about all the different and fun things they had seen.

"I know we couldn't do everything we wanted,

but we only had so much time for such a big and interesting city," said Mom.

"Do you think we should come back again? I'd really like to see some of the art museums."

"I want to come back," said Travis, smiling enthusiastically.

After all his moping at the beginning of their trip,

Travis realized that he really did have a great time—that with their 'new' family of three,

they could still have fun together.

"I want to come back, too," said Jessie,

"but next time, I want to ride one of those huge boats at Navy Pier!"

"Just sit back and relax now," said Mom. "Let's try to have a quiet ride home."

And with that, the hum of the train's wheels slowly lulled the boys to sleep.